NO NONSENSE COOKING GUIDE

# BREAKFASTS & BRUNCHES

NO NONSENSE COOKING GUIDE

# BREAKFASTS & BRUNCHES

## IRENA CHALMERS

LONGMEADOW PRESS

BREAKFASTS & BRUNCHES

Copyright © 1987 by Irena Chalmers

Published by Longmeadow Press, 201 High Ridge Road, Stamford, Connecticut 06904. No part of this book may be reproduced or used in any form or by any means, electronic or mechanical, including photocopying, recording, or by an information storage and retrieval system, without permission in writing from the publisher.

ISBN 0-681-40275-X

Printed in the United States of America

0 9 8 7 6 5 4 3 2 1

## STAFF FOR NO NONSENSE COOKING GUIDES

EDITORIAL DIRECTION: **Jean Atcheson**

MANAGING EDITOR: **Mary Goodbody**

COVER DESIGN: **Karen Skelton**

ART DIRECTION & DESIGN: **Helene Berinsky**

RECIPE DEVELOPMENT: **Elizabeth Wheeler**

ASSISTANT EDITORS: **Mary Dauman, Dorothy Atcheson**

PROJECT MANAGER: **Nancy Kipper**

COVER PHOTOGRAPH: **Gerald Zanetti**

TYPESETTING: **ComCom, Allentown, Pennsylvania**

PRODUCTION SERVICES: **William S. Konecky Associates, New York**

# CONTENTS

**ACKNOWLEDGMENTS**

Grateful acknowledgment is made to Fleischmann's Yeast and Nabisco Brands for permission to reproduce or adapt original recipes.

# BREAKFASTS AND BRUNCHES

The aroma of brewing coffee helps us greet a new day with a sense of anticipation and well-being. Add to this the promise of freshly baked muffins, just-made omelettes, homemade sausage patties, French toast and perhaps some fried potatoes—and the morning meal quickly becomes the best one of the day.

Breakfast has long been a popular meal. In the West, it is often a hearty repast of fried eggs, steak and hash browned potatoes or perhaps thick stacks of buttermilk flapjacks. Southwesterners frequently eat spicy huevos rancheros and refried beans, while Southerners like grits with their eggs and light baking powder biscuits. Northeasterners can be found setting out bagels and cream cheese on the breakfast table, or, more tradition-ally, hot oatmeal or blueberry pancakes with pure maple syrup. Luckily, with our streamlined system of transportation, far-reaching marketing strategies and instant methods of communication, such regional pref-erences need not be confined to a geographic area. Breakfast lovers can enjoy these and other favorites, regardless of where they live.

Breakfast is not the only star of the morning. Brunch, a relatively recent invention, is served later in the day—around noon, give or take an hour—and often includes more elaborate dishes among the expected offerings of bacon, fresh fruit and coffeecakes. Brunch is usually reserved for weekends, for those days when we can afford the time to gather with a few friends for several relaxing daytime hours of good food and good drink. It is also a meal to be enjoyed within the family, providing a chance to unwind with a cup of coffee, a sweet muffin and the Sunday paper.

Whether you are planning a festive breakfast or brunch, keep the preparations simple and unpretentious. Set the table with a bright colored tablecloth and fresh flowers. Put out bowls of fresh fruit and baskets of home-baked breads. Squeeze the orange juice and make sure the coffee is hot and strong. Get up a little early so that you can bake coffeecake, biscuits or muffins. Plan to serve a little more food than perhaps is needed—brunch is a true "grazing" meal when guests like to try a little of this and a little of that, abandoning any concern about eating a savory dish before a sweet one.

Because they are served in the morning, breakfasts and brunches do require planning. Weekend mornings are not the time to dash out for last-minute provisions. Stock up on ice, milk, cream and butter as well as the ingredients for the main dishes. Prepare as much as you can ahead of time. This not only makes serving the meal organized and orderly, but will allow you, too, to relax and enjoy that second cup of coffee and extra slice of banana bread.

# CHAPTER 1

# MUFFINS, QUICK BREADS AND BISCUITS

Muffins and biscuits—quick and easy to mix and bake—make a tremendous difference to a morning meal. Just as the aromas of brewing coffee or sizzling bacon arouse the senses, the scent of baking breads wafting from the kitchen makes everyone in the house eager for the day to begin. Put a basket of napkin-wrapped hot biscuits or muffins or a sliced fruit bread on the table and forget about rounding up the family for breakfast—they will appear as if by magic.

Muffins, biscuits and quick breads are usually leavened with baking powder, which is a combination of acid and alkali. When an acid ingredient, such as sour cream, citrus juice or cranberries, will be part of the batter, baking soda (an alkali) alone is needed. In both cases, the chemical reaction which produces the leavening or raising begins as soon as the dry ingredients are mixed with the wet. Both elements should be combined separately and then mixed together swiftly just before baking.

Most of the actual leavening, in fact, occurs in the heat of the oven, but the necessity to combine the batter fairly rapidly is probably what gives rise to the term "quick bread," which encompasses all the recipes in this chapter. Of course, they are "quick" in other ways, too—speedy to bring to the table and almost instantly eaten up to the very last, delicious crumb.

# Cornbread

Serves 6

Classic cornbread brightens up nearly any meal, whether it is breakfast, brunch or supper.

> 1 cup all-purpose flour
> 1 cup yellow cornmeal
> 1 teaspoon salt
> 4 teaspoons baking powder
> 2 tablespoons sugar
> 1 cup milk
> 1 large egg
> 4 tablespoons (2 ounces) butter, melted

Heat the oven to 425 degrees. Butter an 8-inch-square baking pan.

Combine the flour, cornmeal, salt, baking powder and sugar in a large bowl. Beat the milk and the egg together until blended and pour them over the dry ingredients. Add the melted butter and stir just until the dry ingredients are moistened.

Turn the batter into the prepared pan. Bake for 15 to 20 minutes until the cornbread is firm and golden brown. Cut into squares and serve warm.

# Biscuits

**Makes 16 biscuits**

Hot, just-made biscuits are wonderful on their own but biscuit dough also makes a delicious crumbly crust for a meat or chicken pot pie. Simply cover the ingredients with the rolled biscuit dough 20 minutes before the total cooking time has elapsed.

> *2 cups all-purpose flour*
> *4 teaspoons baking powder*
> *½ teaspoon salt*
> *4 tablespoons (2 ounces) butter, cut into small*
> *    pieces*
> *⅔ cup cold milk*

Heat the oven to 450 degrees.

Combine the flour, baking powder and salt in a large bowl. Add the butter and quickly work it into the flour with your fingertips until the mixture resembles coarse crumbs.

Add the milk and stir gently until the mixture holds together. Press the dough together to form a compact ball.

Turn the dough onto a floured board. Knead it gently 2 or 3 times and then flatten it. Roll the dough out ¼ inch thick and cut into 2-inch rounds, using a biscuit cutter or an inverted glass.

Put the biscuits on an unbuttered baking sheet and bake for 10 minutes. Lower the heat to 350 degrees and continue baking for 5 to 8 minutes longer until golden brown.

You can cut out biscuits as much as an hour before baking if you refrigerate them.

# Sour Cream Orange Biscuits

**Makes 12 biscuits**

A slightly more chewy variation on traditional baking powder biscuits that adds the tang of citrus and sour cream.

> *2 cups sifted all-purpose flour*
> *3 tablespoons brown sugar*
> *1 tablespoon baking powder*
> *½ teaspoon salt*
> *6 tablespoons (3 ounces) butter, chilled and cut into small pieces*
> *½ cup sour cream*
> *¼ cup orange juice*
> *1 tablespoon grated orange rind*

If you have any reason to think your oven temperature may not be accurate, use an oven thermometer when baking. They are obtainable at any supermarket and are quite inexpensive.

Heat the oven to 450 degrees.

Mix the flour, sugar, baking powder and salt in a large bowl. Add the butter and quickly work it into the flour with your fingertips until the mixture resembles coarse meal.

Combine the sour cream, orange juice and orange rind and add to the dry ingredients. Stir the mixture gently until it forms a soft dough. Turn the dough out onto a lightly floured work surface. Knead gently 2 or 3 times and then flatten it. Roll the dough out ½ inch thick and cut into 2-inch rounds, using a cookie cutter or inverted glass.

Put the biscuits on an unbuttered baking sheet. Bake for 12 to 15 minutes until golden brown. Serve hot.

# Popovers

**Makes 8 popovers**

Serve light, airy popovers with butter and fruit preserves. The secret of making great popovers is pouring
the batter into heated, well-oiled tins.

> *2⅓ tablespoons vegetable oil*
> *1 cup all-purpose flour*
> *1 cup milk*
> *2 large eggs*
> *¼ teaspoon salt*

Heat the oven to 450 degrees.

Put ½ teaspoon of vegetable oil in each of 8 muffin
cups or in 8 sections of a muffin tin. Put the tin in the
oven.

Put the flour, milk, eggs, salt and the remaining 1
tablespoon of oil in a blender or food processor, and
blend at high speed for 20 seconds until the batter is
smooth. Turn the blender off and scrape down the sides
of the jar with a rubber spatula. Blend the batter for a
few seconds longer.

Remove the muffin tin from the oven. Pour the batter
into the hot cups, filling them half full. Bake for 30
minutes without opening the oven door until the
popovers are puffed and well browned.

Serve immediately.

# Blueberry Muffins

**Makes 12 muffins**

Always a favorite, and especially good with the tiny wild blueberries you have picked, or found frozen in an enterprising market.

> *1½ cups all-purpose flour*
> *1½ teaspoons baking powder*
> *¼ teaspoon salt*
> *5 tablespoons (2½ ounces) butter, softened*
> *½ cup sugar*
> *1 large egg*
> *½ cup milk*
> *1 teaspoon lemon juice*
> *1 cup fresh blueberries*
>
> TOPPING:
> *⅓ cup sugar*
> *1 tablespoon cinnamon*

Mix muffin batter lightly for muffins with a light and tender texture and a well-rounded dome top.

Heat the oven to 400 degrees. Line a 12-cup muffin tin with paper liners.

Sift together the flour, baking powder and salt.

Beat the butter in a large bowl until creamy. Gradually add the sugar and continue beating until the mixture is fluffy. Beat in the egg. Gradually stir in the flour mixture, alternating with the milk and lemon juice and ending with the flour. Fold in the blueberries.

Spoon the batter into the muffin cups. Mix together the sugar and cinnamon and sprinkle each muffin with a teaspoon of the cinnamon sugar.

Bake the muffins for about 25 minutes. Serve warm.

# Banana Bread

**Makes 1 9-inch loaf**

A warm loaf of banana bread is sweetly satisfying at the breakfast or brunch table. Serve it with or without butter.

Most quick breads—especially those made with fruit and nuts—taste even better if allowed to "age" for a day or two, well wrapped in foil or transparent wrap.

> 2 cups all-purpose flour
> ½ teaspoon salt
> ½ teaspoon baking soda
> 8 tablespoons (4 ounces) butter
> ½ cup packed brown sugar
> 2 tablespoons honey
> 2 large eggs
> 2 ripe bananas, mashed
> ½ cup chopped candied fruit or raisins
> ½ cup chopped walnuts

Heat the oven to 350 degrees. Butter and flour a 9-by-5-inch loaf pan.

Sift the flour, salt and baking soda into a large bowl. Beat the butter and brown sugar with an electric mixer until thick and creamy. Stir in the honey. Add the eggs and beat until fluffy. Add the flour mixture and stir to make a smooth batter.

Fold in the bananas, candied fruit or raisins and walnuts. Turn the batter into the prepared pan. Bake for 1¼ hours, or until a toothpick inserted in the center comes out clean.

Turn the bread out onto a wire rack to cool.

# Cranberry Bread

**Makes 2 9-inch loaves**

A moist, firm-textured bread that slices easily and keeps well, too.

> *3 cups all-purpose flour*
> *2 teaspoons baking soda*
> *2 teaspoons baking powder*
> *1 teaspoon salt*
> *4 tablespoons (2 ounces) butter, melted*
> *4 large eggs*
> *2 cups sugar*
> *1 cup orange juice*
> *2 cups cranberries*
> *1 cup slivered almonds or chopped walnuts*
> *½ cup golden raisins*
> *3½-ounce container (½ cup) glacéed cherries*

Reheat quick breads by wrapping them loosely with foil and putting them in a 250-degree oven for 10 to 15 minutes. Muffins can be reheated in the same way but will take a little less time.

Heat the oven to 350 degrees. Butter and flour 2 9-by-5-inch loaf pans.

Sift together the flour, baking soda, baking powder and salt into a large bowl.

Beat the butter with the eggs in an electric mixer and beat in the sugar. Add the orange juice gradually, alternating with the flour mixture. Fold in the cranberries, nuts, raisins and cherries.

Divide the batter between the pans and smooth the tops. Bake the loaves for 1¼ hours until a toothpick inserted in the center of each loaf comes out clean. Cool the loaves in the pans for 15 minutes and then turn them out to cool on a rack. Wrap the loaves in transparent wrap and set aside for 8 hours before cutting.

# YEAST-RAISED COFFEECAKES, BREADS AND DOUGHNUTS

S earch bakeries, specialty shops and mammoth supermarkets; you will never find bread that tastes as good as the bread you make in your own kitchen. Taking the time to make bread may be a labor of love—but it is a genuinely satisfying one. And the final result is always worth the kneading and rising time, because yeast produces a lighter, tastier product than any other leavening agent. Whether you plan to make several loaves of bread, construct a filled coffee ring for a weekend brunch party or fry light-as-air doughnuts, your family and guests will come back for more—and more.

Yeast needs warmth. During kneading and rising, it releases carbon dioxide gas that becomes trapped in the strands of gluten in the flour. This sequence makes the bread rise. Do not hesitate to knead the bread for as long as the recipe specifies or until the dough reaches the right consistency and appearance. Within obvious boundaries, you cannot "overhandle" yeast dough, as you can pastry dough. Give the dough time to double in bulk (if the recipe instructs you to), and do not try

Store active dry yeast in the refrigerator. Proofing it in warm liquid assures the baker that the yeast is active and triggers its leavening capabilities.

to hurry it. On the other hand, do not let the rising dough sit for much longer than necessary. Many yeast doughs will hold in the refrigerator for several hours or overnight, so you can prepare them in advance up to the time of baking. Already baked (and cooled) yeast breads and coffeecakes also freeze very well—just be sure to take them from the freezer in time to let them reach room temperature slowly before you warm them in a very low oven.

# White Bread

**Makes 1 9-inch loaf**

A single loaf can be made in the food processor, or, if you are kneading by hand, double the recipe to make more bread.

A freshly baked loaf of simple white bread with a golden crust is the ideal accompaniment to any breakfast or brunch—serve it warm from the oven or toasted with sweet butter, fruit preserves, marmalade or honey. It also makes good sandwiches.

> *1 package active dry yeast*
> *½ cup lukewarm water (110 degrees)*
> *½ cup milk*
> *2 tablespoons (1 ounce) butter*
> *1 teaspoon sugar*
> *1 teaspoon salt*
> *3 cups all-purpose flour*
>
> GLAZE:
> *1 large egg yolk*
> *1 tablespoon milk*

Sprinkle the yeast over the surface of the warm water and let stand for 5 minutes until it is foamy on top.

Heat the milk in a small saucepan over low heat and stir in the butter, sugar and salt. When the liquid is hot, remove the saucepan from the heat and let it cool to room temperature. There is no need for the butter to melt completely.

Put the yeast mixture, the cooled milk and the flour in a food processor and process until combined. Continue to process until the dough forms a ball and is smooth, shiny and elastic.

To make the dough by hand, mix the ingredients together in a large bowl with a wooden spoon until the mixture forms a dough. Turn the dough out onto a lightly floured work surface and knead for 8 to 10 minutes until it is smooth, shiny and elastic.

Put the kneaded dough in a lightly oiled bowl. Cover the bowl and leave the dough to rise in a warm place for 1½ hours until doubled in bulk.

Butter a 9-by-5-inch loaf pan (or 2, if you are making double quantities.)

Turn the dough out onto a floured surface and knead it lightly for a few minutes. Shape the dough into a loaf and put it into the prepared pan. Cover loosely with a towel and leave to rise for 1 hour until doubled in bulk.

Heat the oven to 350 degrees.

Combine the egg yolk and milk in a small bowl and beat lightly with a fork. Brush the loaf with the egg wash. Bake the bread for 1 hour until it is golden brown and sounds hollow when tapped.

The ideal environment for rising dough is draft-free with a temperature between 85 and 90 degrees. If your kitchen is a little cooler, it will not matter, but try to keep the dough near the stove or high up where the air is warmer.

### HOW MUCH FLOUR?

The amount of flour in a yeast bread recipe is never exact. How much you will need depends on the type of flour and how it absorbs moisture. Flour—even with the same brand name—varies from region to region around the country.

# Water Bagels

**Makes 1 dozen**

Brunch would not be brunch without bagels. Making them yourself insures the freshness of these gorgeously dense, chewy rolls. Serve them with cream cheese and smoked salmon, cream cheese and chives, butter or jam.

> *4–5 cups all-purpose flour*
> *3 tablespoons sugar*
> *1 tablespoon salt*
> *1 package active dry yeast*
> *1½ cups very warm tap water*
> *1 egg white*
> *1 tablespoon cold water*

Thoroughly mix 1½ cups flour, sugar, salt and yeast in the large bowl of an electric mixer. Gradually add the warm tap water and beat for 2 minutes at medium speed. Scrape down the sides of the bowl every now and then.

Add ½ cup of flour and beat at high speed for 2 minutes. Stir in enough additional flour to make a soft dough. Turn this out onto a lightly floured surface and knead for 8 to 10 minutes until the dough is elastic and smooth.

Put the dough into an ungreased bowl, cover and let it rise in a warm place for 20 minutes. It will *not* double in bulk.

Punch down the dough and turn it out onto a lightly floured surface. Roll it into a 12-by-10-inch rectangle and cut it into 12 equal-sized strips. Pinch the ends of the strips together to form circles. Put the rings on ungreased baking sheets, cover and let rise in a warm place for 20 minutes. The bagels will not double.

Heat the oven to 375 degrees.

Pour water into a large shallow pan to a depth of 1¾

inches and bring to the boil. Reduce the heat and put several bagels into the water. Simmer for 7 minutes, then lift them from the water with a slotted spoon. Cool the bagels on paper towels for 5 minutes and then transfer them to ungreased baking sheets. Repeat the process with all the bagels.

Bake the bagels on their sheets for 10 minutes and then take them from the oven. Combine the egg white and cold water and brush the egg wash over the bagels. Put them back in the oven to bake for another 20 minutes until firm and browned. Cool the bagels on wire racks before serving.

# Cheese-Filled Coffee Ring

**Makes 1 9-inch ring**

A sweet yeast dough enveloping an even sweeter cream cheese filling. Pour a second cup of coffee!

> Yeast bread freezes very successfully; make sure the loaf is completely cooled before wrapping it in foil or freezer paper.

> 2¾–3¼ cups all-purpose flour
> 10 tablespoons sugar
> ¾ teaspoon salt
> 2 packages active dry yeast
> ⅓ cup water
> ⅓ cup milk
> 6 tablespoons (3 ounces) butter
> 2 large eggs
> 3 ounces cream cheese
> ½ teaspoon vanilla extract

Thoroughly mix 1 cup of flour, 6 tablespoons sugar, salt and yeast in the large bowl of an electric mixer.

Combine the water, milk and butter in a saucepan

and heat over very low heat until the mixture is very warm. (The butter does not need to melt completely.) Gradually add the mixture to the dry ingredients and beat for 2 minutes at medium speed.

Add 1 egg and ½ cup flour and beat for 2 minutes at high speed, scraping the bowl occasionally. Stir in enough additional flour to make a soft dough. Cover and let rise in a warm place for about 50 minutes, until doubled in bulk.

Beat the cream cheese in a small bowl until light and fluffy. Add the remaining egg, the remaining 4 tablespoons of sugar and the vanilla, and beat until well blended. Set aside.

Punch down the dough and turn out onto a lightly floured surface. Roll the dough into an 18-inch circle and drape the circle over a 6-cup ring mold. Gently fit the dough into the mold, leaving about a 1-inch overhang. Let the dough cover the center ring.

Pour the cheese filling into the mold. Fold the overhang back over the filling and seal the edges to the inside ring of dough. Cut a cross in the dough extending over the center ring to form 4 triangles. Fold each triangle back over the dough and seal. Cover and let rise in a warm place for about 50 minutes until doubled in bulk.

Heat the oven to 350 degrees. Bake the ring for about 30 minutes until a toothpick inserted in the center comes out clean. Remove the ring from the mold and cool on a wire rack.

# Cinnamon Twist Coffeecake

**Makes 2 9-inch square cakes**

These square coffeecakes look almost as though they are braided. The folded dough is cut into strips, twisted and then arranged in the pans so that the strips touch and thus join together during baking.

> 6–6½ cups all-purpose flour
> 1¼ cups sugar
> 1 teaspoon salt
> 2 packages active dry yeast
> 1 cup milk
> ⅔ cup water
> 8 tablespoons (4 ounces) butter
> 2 large eggs
> ¾ cup dark seedless raisins
> 2 teaspoons cinnamon
> Vegetable oil

Butter 2 9-inch-square baking pans.

Mix together 1¾ cups flour, ½ cup sugar, the salt and the yeast in the large bowl of an electric mixer.

Combine the milk, water and 4 tablespoons of the butter in a saucepan. Heat over low heat until the liquid is warm to the touch (120 to 130 degrees).

Stir the liquid into the dry ingredients and beat for 2 minutes with an electric mixer at medium speed. Add the eggs and ½ cup of flour. Beat the mixture at high speed for 2 minutes, scraping the bowl occasionally. Stir in the raisins and enough additional flour to make a stiff dough.

Turn the dough out onto a lightly floured work surface and knead for 8 to 10 minutes until it is smooth and elastic. Put the dough into a lightly oiled bowl and cover with transparent wrap and then a towel. Let the dough rest for 30 minutes in a warm place.

*(continued on next page)*

Melt the remaining 4 tablespoons of the butter.

Divide the dough in half. Roll out each half into a 12-inch square and brush lightly with melted butter.

Combine the remaining ¾ cup of the sugar with the cinnamon. Sprinkle the center third of each square with 3 tablespoons of the sugar mixture. Fold one third of the dough over the center third. Brush the top of the folded section lightly with melted butter and sprinkle with 3 tablespoons of the sugar mixture. Fold the remaining third of the dough over the 2 layers and press gently. Repeat with the second piece of dough.

Cut the folded pieces of dough crosswise into strips about 1 inch wide. Take hold of the ends of each strip and and twist tightly in opposite directions. Seal the ends together firmly and arrange the strips next to each other in the prepared pans. Cover loosely with wax paper that has been brushed lightly with vegetable oil, and then cover tightly with transparent wrap. Refrigerate for 2 to 24 hours.

Heat the oven to 375 degrees.

Take the pans from the refrigerator, remove the wrappings carefully and let stand for 15 minutes.

Bake the coffeecakes for 30 to 35 minutes until well risen and browned. Allow the cakes to cool in the pans for 5 minutes, and then remove from the pans and cool on wire racks.

# Beignets

**Serves 8**

In New Orleans, you can buy these warm sugary puffs from street vendors at any time of the day or night and the strong chicory-flavored local coffee tastes marvelous with them.

*1 cup water*
*4 tablespoons butter, cut into small pieces*
*¼ teaspoon salt*
*1 cup sifted all-purpose flour*
*4 eggs*
*Oil, for deep-frying*
*Confectioners' sugar, for dusting*

APRICOT SAUCE:
*8-ounce jar apricot preserves*
*1 tablespoon lemon juice*

Pour the water into a saucepan and bring to the boil. Add the butter and salt. When the butter is melted, remove the pan from the heat and add the flour all at once. Return the pan to low heat and stir vigorously with a wooden spoon for 2 minutes until the mixture is smooth and shiny and forms a ball.

Remove the pan from the heat and beat in the eggs one at a time, beating after each addition, until the mixture is smooth.

Heat the oil to 375 degrees. Using 2 tablespoons, drop mounds of the mixture into the deep fat. Do not crowd the pan or the puffs will not crisp. As they cook, the puffs will expand and roll over on the surface of the fat. Cook for about 3 minutes, until crisp. Drain on paper towels and dust with confectioners' sugar.

Heat the apricot preserves in a small saucepan. Add the lemon juice and stir until smooth. Serve on the side as a sauce for the beignets.

# Yeast-Raised Jelly Doughnuts

Makes about 3 dozen

Name one child who does not like jelly doughnuts. And now name one adult.

> 1 cup milk
> 2 tablespoons sugar
> 1 teaspoon salt
> 4 tablespoons (2 ounces) butter, cut into
>     small pieces
> 2 packages active dry yeast
> 3½ cups sifted all-purpose flour
> 2 large eggs, lightly beaten
> Oil or solid shortening for deep-frying
> 2 cups (approximately) fruit jelly, for filling
> Confectioners' sugar, for dusting

Heat the milk over moderate heat until it comes to a simmer. Pour ½ cup of the milk into a bowl and stir in the sugar, salt and butter. Stir until the butter has melted and let the mixture cool to slightly warmer than body temperature, about 100 degrees.

Cool the remaining ½ cup of the milk to 100 degrees and pour it into another bowl. Sprinkle the yeast over the milk and set aside for 5 minutes until it is bubbly and foamy.

Sift the flour into a large bowl. Add both bowls of milk and the lightly beaten eggs and stir until the mixture forms a dough. Turn the dough out onto a lightly floured surface and knead lightly for 8 to 10 minutes, adding a little more flour if necessary to form a smooth dough. Put the dough in an oiled bowl, cover with transparent wrap and leave in a warm place for 1½ hours until doubled in bulk.

Roll the dough out to a thickness of ½ inch and cut

circles with a cookie cutter or inverted glass. Put the pieces of dough on a lightly floured surface and cover again for 1 hour or until doubled in bulk.

Heat the oil or shortening to 375 degrees.

Fry the doughnuts a few at a time for about 4 minutes, turning them constantly so that they brown evenly. Remove them to wire racks lined with paper towels to cool. Repeat the process until all the doughnuts have been fried.

Fit a large pastry bag with a number 6 tube and fill with the jelly. Insert the pastry tube into each doughnut and fill each in turn with a generous tablespoon or so of jelly. Dust the doughnuts with confectioners' sugar just before serving.

# CHAPTER 3

# EGG AND CHEESE DISHES

When there is a sense of leisure to think about breakfast or brunch, eggs will invariably come to mind—and very pleasantly too. A kitchen staple, along with butter, sugar and flour, they are sure to be on hand, and can be served in a multitude of ways. Fried eggs on toast, three-minute boiled eggs and scrambled eggs with bacon are common breakfast fare and always welcome, but with a few more ingredients you can create breakfast and brunch dishes to please the most discriminating guest or finicky family member.

Eggs and cheese are a natural pairing, too, especially fresh cheese, which has a soft texture and mild flavor that blend admirably with the similar characteristics of eggs. Fresh cheeses are, simply, unaged and uncured cheeses such as cream cheese, farmer's cheese, ricotta, mozzarella and some chèvres. Whatever recipe you choose, cook the eggs and cheese gently and attentively; both are fragile but will reward you generously for a little tender care.

# Creamy Scrambled Eggs

**Serves 4 to 6**

No breakfast—or brunch—is complete without scrambled eggs, the creamier the better. Be sure to cook the eggs over low heat, and stir them constantly for a really smooth result.

> *3 tablespoons (1½ ounces) butter*
> *8 large eggs, lightly beaten*
> *4 ounces cream cheese, cut into small pieces*
> *1 tablespoon finely chopped parsley*
> *Salt*
> *Pepper*

Melt the butter in a heavy saucepan over low heat. Add the eggs, cream cheese, parsley and salt and pepper to taste. Cook, stirring, until the eggs form soft curds. Taste and adjust the seasoning. Serve immediately with hot buttered toast.

### TIPS ABOUT EGGS

The best way to cook eggs in their shells to a firm consistency is to put the eggs in boiling water, boil them for 2 to 3 minutes and then turn off the heat (or remove the pan from the stove) and let the eggs sit in the hot water for about 10 minutes.

Always cook eggs gently over low heat—scrambling eggs or cooking omelettes over high heat causes the proteins to separate, resulting in watery eggs.

You can store eggs for up to a month in the refrigerator in their cartons. The cardboard carton shields the shells and keeps the eggs fresh longer than the refrigerator egg keeper.

# Omelette with Herbs and Chicken

Serves 2

This omelette makes a good quick meal.

> *3 tablespoons (1½ ounces) butter*
> *½ cup chopped cooked chicken*
> *½ teaspoon celery seed*
> *4 large eggs*
> *½ teaspoon salt*
> *2 tablespoons finely chopped parsley*
> *1 tablespoon chopped chives*
> *1 teaspoon chopped fresh tarragon or*
> *   ¼ teaspoon dried*
> *Pepper*

An omelette pan should be 9 inches in diameter with rounded sides and a heavy bottom. Non-stick surfaces are helpful.

Heat 1 tablespoon of butter in a small skillet over moderate heat. Add the chicken and celery seed and cook, stirring, until the chicken is very hot.

Combine the eggs, salt, parsley, chives, tarragon and pepper to taste in a bowl. Beat with a fork until all the ingredients are well combined.

Heat the remaining 2 tablespoons of butter in a non-stick 9-inch skillet or omelette pan over medium-high heat until it is foaming. Reduce the heat to moderate and add the eggs. Stir with a wooden fork held flat, as if preparing scrambled eggs. Continue stirring until the eggs are almost set and form a smooth layer on the pan's surface.

Add the hot chicken in a line across the pan on the side opposite the handle. Tilt the pan away from you. Slide a spatula under the side nearest the handle and fold the omelette in half. Slide the folded omelette to the center of the pan and brown the underside for 30 seconds. Invert the pan on top of a warm serving plate. Cut the omelette in half and serve immediately.

# Spicy Shirred Egg Casserole

**Serves 6**

A full-flavored and easy-to-make egg casserole. If you cannot find hot sausage sold in bulk, buy links of hot Italian or Polish sausage and remove the casings.

> *¾ cup Tomato Sauce (see page 63)*
> *6 large eggs*
> *Salt*
> *Pepper*
> *1 pound hot Italian sausage, cooked, drained and crumbled*
> *2–3 scallions, thinly sliced*
> *1 cup sour cream, at room temperature*
> *½ cup fresh bread crumbs*
> *1½ cups grated sharp cheddar or Monterey jack cheese*

Heat the oven to 425 degrees.

Butter a large shallow 9-inch casserole. Spread the tomato sauce evenly over the bottom of the dish. Break the eggs carefully onto the tomato sauce and season with salt and pepper to taste.

Sprinkle the crumbled sausage and the scallions over the eggs. Spoon the sour cream evenly over the sausage. Combine the bread crumbs with the cheese and sprinkle them evenly over the sour cream.

Bake the casserole in the oven for 10 to 12 minutes until the eggs are set and the cheese is melted.

# Huevos Rancheros

**Serves 4**

One of the many joys of visiting Mexico is to awaken with the anticipation of spicy huevos rancheros for breakfast. The piquant flavors start any day right—on either side of the border.

> *8 3-inch corn tortillas*
> *6 tablespoons (3 ounces) butter*
> *½ cup finely chopped onion*
> *2 green peppers, seeded and chopped*
> *Salt*
> *8 large eggs*
> *1½ cups hot Tomato Sauce (see page 63)*
> *1½ cups hot Refried Beans (see page 55)*

Heat the oven to 300 degrees. Wrap the tortillas tightly in aluminum foil and heat them in the oven. Keep them warm until ready to use.

Melt 3 tablespoons of butter in a large skillet over moderate heat. Add the chopped onion and green peppers and cook, stirring, for 10 minutes until soft and translucent. Season with salt to taste.

Heat the remaining 3 tablespoons of butter in another large skillet over moderate heat until bubbling. Fry the eggs to the desired doneness.

Put 2 tortillas on each plate and cover with part of the onion and green peppers. Top with 2 eggs. Spoon the tomato sauce over the eggs and serve the refried beans on the side.

# Golden-Fried Ham and Cheese Sandwiches

**Makes 6 servings or about 48 hors d'oeuvres**

To make these sandwiches special, use fresh Italian bread, paper-thin slices of prosciutto and a fresh, creamy mozzarella. Cut into bite-sized pieces, the sandwiches are good to serve with drinks. They are always served hot.

*12 thin slices of bread, crusts removed*
*¼ pound prosciutto or other thinly sliced ham*
*½ pound mozzarella or similar fast-melting, semi-soft cheese, chopped or grated*
*1 tablespoon olive oil*
*1 teaspoon dried marjoram*
*3 large eggs, lightly beaten*
*3 tablespoons milk*
*1½ cups all-purpose flour*
*Vegetable oil, for deep-frying*

Freshly made mozzarella cheese is sold at many Italian markets and cheese stores. Ask about it the next time you visit the cheese shop—it is far superior to the packaged kind.

Make 6 sandwiches with the bread and equal amounts of the meat and cheese, leaving a small border of bread. Before putting the top piece of bread on the sandwich, sprinkle the cheese with a drop of oil and a light scattering of marjoram. Press the edges of the bread together to form a seal.

Beat the eggs and milk together in a shallow dish. Spread the flour in another shallow dish.

Heat 2 to 3 inches of oil to 375 degrees in a large skillet over moderate heat. Dredge the sandwiches lightly with the flour and dip them into the egg and milk mixture so that the bread absorbs the egg mixture. Fry 2 sandwiches at a time for about 2 minutes on each side until golden. Drain on a wire rack lined with a double thickness of paper towels and serve immediately.

# Quiche Lorraine

**Serves 6 to 8**

Quiches of all kinds have long been a popular brunch or lunch dish. This is the classic that started the "quiche craze"—and it is still the all-time favorite.

QUICHE PASTRY:
*1¼ cups sifted all-purpose flour*
*⅛ teaspoon salt*
*4 tablespoons (2 ounces) butter, chilled and cut into small pieces*
*2 tablespoons (1 ounce) solid vegetable shortening, chilled*
*3–4 tablespoons cold water*

FILLING:
*½ pound bacon, cooked until crisp, crumbled*
*1 cup (6 ounces) Swiss or Gruyère cheese, grated*
*4 large eggs*
*1 tablespoon all-purpose flour*
*1½ cups heavy cream, light cream or half-and-half*
*⅛ teaspoon salt*
*⅛ teaspoon ground nutmeg*
*⅛ teaspoon pepper*
*1 tablespoon (½ ounce) butter, melted*

To make the pastry, combine the flour and salt in a large bowl. Add the butter and shortening and toss lightly, then rub them into the flour with your fingertips or a pastry blender until the mixture is crumbly.

Add 3 tablespoons of cold water and stir with a fork, adding more water if necessary to make the dough come together. Gather the dough together and form into a ball. Press it lightly into a disc shape, wrap in wax paper or transparent wrap and chill in the refrigerator for at least 30 minutes.

Heat the oven to 350 degrees.

Roll the dough out on a floured work surface into a 12-inch circle about ⅛ inch thick. Brush off the excess flour and fit the circle into a 10-inch pie plate. Turn the dough under around the edge and crimp it. Cover the pastry with a lightly oiled piece of aluminum foil and weight with a layer of dried beans or rice.

Bake the pastry for 15 minutes to set it. Carefully remove the foil and beans and increase the oven temperature to 375 degrees.

Scatter the crumbled bacon and the grated cheese in the partially baked pie shell.

Combine the eggs, flour, cream and seasonings in a bowl, stirring with a wire whisk. Pour the mixture into the pie shell over the bacon and cheese. Pour the melted butter on top of the custard.

Bake the quiche for 35 minutes until the custard is puffy and golden brown on top. Allow it to cool slightly and serve it warm.

# Zucchini Quiche

Serves 6 to 8

The filling for this quiche can also be served as a separate vegetable dish. Other fresh vegetables such as yellow squash, peppers or mushrooms can be substituted for the zucchini.

>*Quiche Pastry (see page 34)*
>*2 tablespoons olive oil*
>*¼ cup finely chopped parsley*
>*2 cloves garlic, finely chopped*
>*1 pound small zucchini, trimmed and thinly sliced*
>*Salt*
>*Pepper*
>*¾ cup bread crumbs*
>*¾ cup grated Swiss or Gruyère cheese*
>*2 large eggs, lightly beaten*
>*¾ cup milk or light cream*
>*¼ cup grated parmesan cheese*

Prepare and partially bake the pastry according to the directions on page 34. Remove it from the oven and carefully lift off the foil and beans. Increase the oven temperature to 400 degrees.

Heat the oil in a skillet over medium-high heat and cook the parsley, garlic and zucchini until the zucchini is lightly browned and softened. Remove from the heat and season to taste with salt and pepper.

Layer the zucchini mixture, bread crumbs and Swiss cheese in the partially baked pastry shell.

Combine the eggs with the milk or cream in a bowl, stirring with a wire whisk. Pour the mixture over the vegetables in the pie shell. Sprinkle the surface with the parmesan cheese. Bake for 25 minutes until the custard is puffy and golden brown on top. Serve warm.

# CHAPTER 4

# HASH AND OTHER SAVORY DISHES

**B**reakfast is not only a time for eggs—meat and fish have their very definite place at the table. In fact, many a breakfast lover feels slightly "cheated" if a sizable or celebratory morning meal does not include corned beef hash, spicy pork sausage or a delicate fish or shrimp dish. A well made hash is a straightforward treat and is a splendid way of using up tasty leftovers.

Brunch, by its nature usually served a little later in the day than breakfast, is a good time to offer Tex-Mex and Mexican food. Food conceived in the land of sunshine seems a natural for the sunniest time of day, and goes naturally with Bloody Marys and other brunchtime drinks.

# Corned Beef Hash

**Serves 4 to 6**

The saltiness of corned beef is offset to perfection by the cabbage and potatoes in this most famous of all hashes.

Hash is a combination of (mostly) already cooked foods. Its name is derived from the French word *hâcher*, which means "to chop."

*1 pound corned beef*
*1 medium-size onion, chopped*
*2 cups thinly sliced cabbage, cooked and well*
    *drained, chopped*
*2 large boiling potatoes, cooked, peeled and grated*
*¼ cup tomato puree*
*½ teaspoon salt*
*Pepper*
*2 tablespoons oil*

Chop the corned beef finely by hand or in a food processor and put it in a large bowl. Add the onion, cabbage, potatoes, tomato puree, salt and pepper to taste, and mix well.

Heat the oil in a large skillet over moderate heat. Add the corned beef mixture, shaping it in the pan into a flat cake. Cook the hash until it is hot and the underside is well browned. Invert the cake onto a plate and slide it back into the pan to brown the other side. Cut into wedges to serve.

# Chicken Hash

**Serves 4 to 6**

A classic white sauce coats the chopped chicken and the mushrooms, while the sherry adds richness to the flavor.

> 3 tablespoons (1½ ounces) butter
> 1 scallion, finely chopped
> ¼ pound mushrooms, thinly sliced
> 2 tablespoons all-purpose flour
> 1½ cups hot milk
> 3 cups chopped cooked chicken
> 1 tablespoon sherry
> ¼ teaspoon salt
> Pepper
> ½ teaspoon poultry seasoning
> ⅓ cup fresh bread crumbs
> ½ cup grated parmesan cheese

Heat the oven to 350 degrees.

Melt 2 tablespoons of butter in a saucepan over high heat. Add the scallion and mushrooms and cook for 5 minutes, stirring often, until the mushrooms have lost their moisture. Add the flour and cook, stirring, for 2 minutes.

Add the milk to the saucepan and stir constantly until the sauce is thickened and smooth.

Add the chicken and sherry to the sauce and season to taste with salt, pepper and poultry seasoning.

Transfer the ingredients to a buttered casserole large enough to hold the hash comfortably. Combine the bread crumbs with the cheese and sprinkle them over the top. Dot the surface of the hash with the remaining butter and bake, uncovered, for 20 minutes until the chicken is hot and the crust is crisp and browned.

# Homemade Sausage Patties

**Makes 2 pounds**

The best sausage you can serve for breakfast or brunch. These patties taste even better if they are permitted to age, unwrapped, in the refrigerator for a day or so to give the flavors time to develop.

> *2 pounds boneless fresh pork, such as pork loin,*
> *pork butt, or shoulder, with the fat*
> *½ cup finely chopped onion*
> *¼ cup finely chopped parsley*
> *1 teaspoon sage*
> *1½ teaspoons salt*
> *1 teaspoon pepper*

Trim the pork of any tough sinews and cut it into 1-inch pieces. Grind the pork in a food processor until it is finely chopped but still has some texture, or put it through a meat grinder fitted with the medium-sized blade.

Pork, and any other meat, will chop or grind more easily if it is chilled in the freezer until firm but not frozen.

Add the onion, parsley, sage, and salt and pepper and mix well. Form the sausage into patties about ½ inch thick.

Fry the patties in a skillet over moderate heat until they are well browned on both sides.

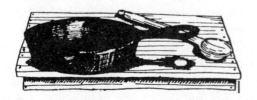

# Chicken Livers with Madeira Sauce

Serves 4

These chicken livers are especially good spooned over hot buttered toast or with freshly cooked rice or pasta.

*3 tablespoons (1½ ounces) butter*
*½ cup finely chopped onion*
*1½ pounds chicken livers*
*Salt and pepper*
*1½ tablespoons flour*
*1 teaspoon paprika*
*¾ cup beef broth*
*¼ cup heavy cream*
*2 tablespoons Madeira or sherry*
*2 tablespoons finely chopped parsley*

Melt the butter in a large skillet over moderate heat. Add the onion and cook, stirring, for 3 to 4 minutes until softened.

Rinse the chicken livers and trim them of all fat and membrane. Cut them in half and dry them on paper towels.

Increase the heat under the skillet to medium-high. Cook the livers in 3 batches to the desired doneness and remove them to a plate. Season with salt and pepper to taste.

Add the flour and paprika to the pan and cook, stirring, for 1 minute. Gradually add the beef broth, cream and Madeira, stirring with a whisk. Reduce the heat to low and cook gently for 5 minutes.

Return the livers to the pan, add the parsley and cook gently just until they are hot. Adjust the seasoning and serve.

# Tacos with Chicken and Potatoes

**Makes 12**

You can make
your own taco
shells by
deep-frying 6-inch
corn tortillas,
holding each one
with tongs in the
familiar folded
shape as it fries.

*2 tablespoons vegetable oil*
*1 clove garlic, chopped*
*½ cup finely chopped onion*
*½ teaspoon ground cumin*
*½ cup chopped canned tomatoes*
*2 medium-size potatoes, cooked, peeled and sliced*
    *⅛ inch thick*
*2–3 canned chilies (serrano or jalapeño), rinsed,*
    *seeded and chopped*
*3–4 cups chopped cooked chicken*
*Salt and pepper*
*12 taco shells*

GARNISH:
*1 cup shredded crisp lettuce*
*1½ cups grated mild cheddar or Monterey jack*
    *cheese*
*Sour cream*
*Taco sauce*

Heat the oil in a large skillet over moderate heat. Add the garlic and chopped onion and cook, stirring, for 2 to 3 minutes. Add the cumin, tomatoes, potatoes and chilies and cook, stirring gently so as not to break up the potatoes, for 5 minutes. Add the chicken and stir gently to combine. Cook for 5 minutes until the mixture is fairly dry. Season with salt and pepper to taste.

Fill the taco shells with the chicken mixture. Serve the lettuce, cheese, sour cream and taco sauce separately in bowls so that everyone can garnish their own tacos.

# Tostados with Shrimp and Crabmeat

**Makes 4 servings**

There are no hard-and-fast rules for tostados—their success depends only on how you combine the ingredients you have on hand and on your own creativity. This combination is pleasingly tasty.

*2 tablespoons vegetable shortening*
*4 corn tortillas*
*2 cups hot Refried Beans (see page 55)*
*6 radishes, thinly sliced*
*4 scallions, thinly sliced*
*1 avocado, peeled, pitted and mashed*
*Juice of 1 lime*
*1 teaspoon salt*
*2–3 drops hot pepper sauce*
*½ pound shrimp, cooked and peeled*
*½ pound lump crabmeat*
*1 cup Tomato Sauce (see page 63)*
*4 iceberg lettuce leaves, shredded*
*12 cherry tomatoes, halved*
*12 pitted black olives*

Heat the shortening in a skillet over medium-high heat and fry each tortilla in turn until crisp and golden.

Put a tortilla on each serving plate. Spread a layer of beans on each and sprinkle with the sliced radishes and scallions.

Mix together the avocado, lime juice, salt and hot pepper sauce and spread a layer on top of the beans.

Combine the shrimp and crabmeat with the tomato sauce and mound on top of the avocado. Garnish each tortilla with shredded lettuce, tomatoes and olives.

# Country Pâté

Makes a 2-quart terrine or casserole

A rich and creamy pâté with a pleasantly rough texture and a lot of flavor is a good addition to a brunch buffet, particularly if there are many light dishes and a variety of breads.

If you prefer, you can remove the bacon slices before serving.

> *½ pound thinly sliced bacon*
> *1 pound ground veal*
> *1 pound ground pork*
> *½ pound ground beef*
> *½ pound ground calves' liver*
> *1 teaspoon dried thyme*
> *1 teaspoon dried sage*
> *¼ teaspoon ground nutmeg*
> *1½ teaspoons salt*
> *Pepper*
> *¼ cup Madeira*
> *¼ cup brandy*
> *¼ cup heavy cream*
> *2 large eggs, lightly beaten*

Heat the oven to 350 degrees.

Line the bottom and sides of the terrine or casserole with three-quarters of the bacon slices. Put the meats into a large bowl and stir in the remaining ingredients.

Spoon the mixture into the terrine or casserole, pressing it down lightly, and cover with the remaining bacon slices. Cover with a lid or aluminum foil. Set the terrine in a larger container such as a roasting pan and add sufficient simmering water to come three-quarters of the way up the sides of the terrine. Bake for 1½ hours.

Remove the lid and cover the pâté with aluminum foil. Allow it to cool and then weight it with kitchen weights or cans of food.

Chill for 48 hours before serving.

# CHAPTER 5

# CRÊPES, PANCAKES, WAFFLES AND FRENCH TOAST

Hot from the skillet or waffle iron, with a pat or two of melting butter mingling with thick, pure maple syrup or crunchy cinnamon sugar, pancakes and waffles are a morning extravaganza. Just as seductive are crispy slices of golden French toast, or paper-thin crêpes wrapped around a sweet filling. These hot cakes of the morning are the way to start the day.

All are a mixture, to some degree, of eggs, milk, flour and sugar, and simple to assemble. The batter can be whipped up in a food processor or by hand in minutes. You can use it at once or let it sit in the refrigerator until the time is right.

Served with the maple syrup you have been hoarding since your last visit to New England, or the homemade strawberry preserves your aunt sent you last Christmas, and a generous amount of sweet butter, hot cakes of all descriptions make a sensational breakfast or brunch centerpiece.

# Crêpes

Makes about 24 crêpes

To make crêpes even thinner and more delicate, use a liquid mixture of half milk and half water. If you are making crêpes for the first time, it is a good idea to use only milk as it makes the batter a little easier to handle.

> *1½ cups milk*
> *3 large eggs*
> *3 tablespoons (1½ ounces) butter, melted*
> *1½ cups sifted all-purpose flour*
> *¼ teaspoon salt*
> *Vegetable oil*

Crêpe batter can be stored in the refrigerator for up to 48 hours. It will thicken as it stands, so you will need to thin it with milk until it is the consistency of light cream.

Put the milk, eggs and melted butter in a food processor. Add the flour and salt and process on high speed until smooth. Let the batter rest, covered, for at least 2 hours before using.

Alternatively, put the flour and salt in a large bowl, add the eggs and stir with a wire whisk until the mixture is blended. Gradually add the milk, whisking until the mixture is smooth. Stir in the melted butter and let it rest, covered, for at least 2 hours.

To prepare the crêpes, heat 1 tablespoon of vegetable oil in a seasoned 5-inch crêpe pan over moderate heat. Pour the oil out and rub the pan with a crumpled piece of paper towel, leaving only a thin film of oil in the pan. Keep the paper towel to rub the pan clean between cooking the crêpes.

Pour about 2 tablespoons of the batter into the pan and roll it around quickly to cover the surface evenly. Pour any excess batter back into the bowl. Only a thin film of batter should remain in the pan.

Cook the crêpe for 30 to 40 seconds until the edges begin to curl and brown and the batter has lost its shine.

Turn it onto the other side and cook for 30 seconds until that side is lightly speckled with browned spots. (It will not brown as evenly as the first side.)

Remove the crêpe to a plate or kitchen towel and repeat the process. Stir the batter from time to time, as it tends to become thicker at the bottom.

As they are cooked, stack the crêpes with the second, speckled side up, so they will be ready for filling. They will not stick together.

# Chicken Crêpes

**Serves 8**

Serve this with a green salad of soft lettuces and a light lemony dressing.

*3 tablespoons (1½ ounces) butter*
*4 scallions, finely chopped*
*1½ cups chopped cooked chicken*
*4 slices crisply cooked bacon, crumbled*
*2 tablespoons finely chopped parsley*
*Salt*
*Pepper*
*16 Crêpes*
*1½ cups hot Cheese Sauce (see page 65)*

Heat the oven to 375 degrees.

Heat 1 tablespoon of the butter in a skillet over moderate heat. Add the scallions and cook, stirring, for 1 minute, until softened. Add the chicken and cook, stirring, until hot. Remove from the heat, stir in the bacon and parsley and season with salt and pepper to taste. *(continued on next page)*

Divide the chicken mixture among the crêpes. Roll each crêpe into a cylinder and arrange, seam side down, in a buttered baking dish large enough to hold them in a single layer. Dot the crêpes with the remaining butter and cover with aluminum foil. Bake in the oven for 15 minutes until hot. Cover with hot cheese sauce and serve immediately.

# Strawberry Crêpes

**Serves 8**

You can cook crêpes ahead, stack with wax paper between each one, cover with transparent wrap and refrigerate for a day or two.

Perfect crêpes need no more embellishment than a little lemon juice and sugar. But they also make a light, delicate wrapping for sweet or savory fillings.

> 2 cups sliced strawberries
> 2 tablespoons sugar
> 1-pound jar strawberry preserves
> 2 tablespoons Grand Marnier
> 24 Crêpes (see page 46)
> 2 tablespoons brandy

Gently toss the sliced strawberries with the sugar and set aside.

Heat the preserves in a small saucepan over low heat until hot. Stir in the Grand Marnier. Spread about a tablespoon of the preserves on the speckled side of each crêpe and fold into a triangle. Arrange the crêpes, slightly overlapping, in a buttered baking dish large enough to hold them in one layer.

Heat the brandy in a small saucepan. Light it with a long match and carefully pour the flaming liquid over the crêpes.

Serve immediately with the sweetened strawberries spooned over the crêpes.

# Cottage Cheese Pancakes

**Serves 4 to 6**

Serve these wonderfully soft, tangy pancakes piping hot with a choice of accompaniments—sour cream, yogurt, fresh fruit, preserves, honey or applesauce.

> *4 large eggs, separated*
> *1½ cups small curd cottage cheese, drained*
> *½ cup all-purpose flour*
> *1 teaspoon baking powder*
> *⅛ teaspoon salt*
> *1 tablespoon sugar*
> *¼ teaspoon cinnamon*
> *¼ teaspoon grated lemon rind (optional)*
> *Vegetable oil*

Beating egg whites before folding them into pancake batter makes the cooked pancakes especially light and fluffy.

Combine the egg yolks, cottage cheese, flour, baking powder, salt, sugar, cinnamon and lemon rind in a large bowl and beat well.

Beat the egg whites with an electric mixer or a wire whisk until stiff peaks form. Fold the whites gently into the batter.

Heat a griddle or skillet over moderate heat until hot. Add a teaspoon of oil, heat for 1 minute and blot the excess with a paper towel.

Drop the batter by large spoonfuls onto the hot griddle or skillet and cook for about 1½ minutes until golden brown. Flip the pancakes carefully and cook until golden brown on the second side. Continue until all the batter is used, adding more oil as necessary.

# Cornmeal Pancakes with Blueberries

Serves 4 to 6

The sweetness of blueberries is a good foil for the definite flavor of cornmeal. Serve the pancakes hot with butter and warmed syrup.

> 1½ cups sifted all-purpose flour
> ¾ cup cornmeal
> 2 tablespoons sugar
> 1 teaspoon baking powder
> ½ teaspoon salt
> 2 cups milk
> 3 large eggs
> 3 tablespoons (1½ ounces) butter, melted
> Corn or vegetable oil
> 1 cup fresh or frozen blueberries

Pancake and waffle batter will hold in the refrigerator for several hours before cooking.

Combine the flour, cornmeal, sugar, baking powder and salt in a large bowl.

Combine the milk and eggs in another bowl and beat well with a wire whisk. Stir in the melted butter. Add the liquid to the dry ingredients, stirring just until the batter is smooth.

Heat a griddle or large skillet over moderate heat until hot. Add a teaspoon of oil, heat for 1 minute and blot the excess with a paper towel.

For each pancake, pour about 4 tablespoons of the batter onto the hot griddle and sprinkle with 1 tablespoon of blueberries. Cook until the edges of the pancakes look dry and the underside is brown. Turn the pancake once and cook until the second side is brown. Continue until all the batter is used, adding more oil to the pan as necessary.

# Sour Cream Waffles

**Serves 4 to 6 (depending on the size of the waffle iron)**

Light and delicate waffles such as these are equally
delicious with butter and maple syrup or with fresh
fruit and a decadent amount of whipped cream.

> *1½ cups sifted all-purpose flour*
> *4 teaspoons baking powder*
> *¼ teaspoon salt*
> *4 large eggs, separated*
> *3 tablespoons sugar*
> *1½ cups sour cream, at room temperature*

Sift the flour, baking powder and salt together into
a large bowl.

Beat the egg yolks with the sugar until slightly thickened. Add the sour cream and beat well. Add the flour
mixture and stir until smooth.

Beat the egg whites with an electric mixer or with a
whisk until stiff peaks form. Fold the whites into the
batter. Refrigerate the batter until ready to use.

Heat the waffle iron until it is hot and a drop of water
flicked onto the iron evaporates instantly. Pour some
batter on the hot iron and cook until nicely browned.
Lift the waffle from the iron and continue making
waffles with the remaining batter. Serve immediately.

# French Toast

Serves 4

A classic breakfast dish—and no wonder. Try this rich version with syrup, honey, preserves or a mixture of cinnamon and sugar.

> *3 large eggs*
> *2 tablespoons confectioners' sugar*
> *½ teaspoon cinnamon*
> *1 teaspoon grated lemon rind*
> *1½ cups milk*
> *½ teaspoon vanilla extract*
> *1–2 tablespoons butter*
> *8 slices firm bread*
> *Butter*

Combine the eggs, confectioners' sugar, cinnamon, lemon rind, milk and vanilla in a large shallow dish and beat well with a wire whisk.

Dip the slices of bread in the egg and milk mixture and allow them to absorb the liquid.

Heat a tablespoon of butter in a large heavy skillet over moderate heat until foaming. Cook the egg-soaked bread in the hot butter until golden brown on both sides. Add more butter if necessary. Serve immediately.

# Chocolate French Toast with Raspberry Sauce

Serves 4

It is never too early in the day for chocolate. When you team it with French toast and raspberry sauce, the fans will come running. Substitute milk chocolate for semi-sweet if you like.

*8 slices white sandwich bread*
*Raspberry preserves*
*5 ounces semisweet chocolate, grated*
*3 large eggs*
*2 tablespoons confectioners' sugar*
*½ teaspoon vanilla extract*
*1½ cups milk*
*1–2 tablespoons (½–1 ounce) butter*

RASPBERRY SAUCE:
*10-ounce package frozen raspberries, defrosted*
*4 tablespoons red currant jelly*
*1 tablespoon orange juice*

Spread 4 slices of the bread with raspberry preserves. Sprinkle an even layer of the grated chocolate over the preserves. Cover with the remaining slices of bread, pressing the edges together to form a seal.

Combine the eggs, confectioners' sugar, vanilla and milk in a large shallow dish. Beat well with a wire whisk.

Carefully dip both sides of the chocolate sandwiches into the egg and milk mixture, making sure they do not come apart. Let each side sit in the liquid long enough to absorb a good deal of it.

Heat a tablespoon of butter in a large skillet over moderate heat until foaming. Cook the sandwiches until they are golden brown on both sides. Add more butter if necessary.

Combine the raspberry sauce ingredients in a saucepan over moderate heat. Stir until the jelly has melted and the mixture is hot. Pass the sauce through a sieve, rubbing the pulp against the sieve with a rubber spatula to extract all the liquid. Discard the seeds. Serve with the warm chocolate French toast.

# CHAPTER 6

# VEGETABLE AND FRUIT SIDE DISHES

Weekend brunch is supposed to be a purely pleasurable meal where regard for calories and conventions can be relegated to more "serious" weekdays. You might serve eggs *and* sausage *and* muffins *and* fried potatoes *and* a sweet fruit dish, or even two. Your guests will revel in the abundance and choice, from deep-fried fritters to a sweet fruit fool or betty.

The dishes described in this chapter are truly extraneous to a balanced meal—and truly delicious and tempting. After all, nobody minds being tempted once in a while; they can always say "No." But if you cook these recipes with love and care, the answer will probably be "Yes, please!"

# Refried Beans

55

VEGETABLE AND
FRUIT SIDE DISHES

**Serves 6**

Refried beans are served at almost every meal in Mexico. For this very basic (and very good) recipe, the beans do not need to be soaked overnight but do require long, slow cooking before they are mashed. Serve these beans with eggs, sausages or any spicy dish.

> 1 pound dry pinto, red kidney or black beans
> 1 large onion, chopped
> 10 cups cold water
> 6 tablespoons lard or vegetable oil
> 1 tablespoon salt

Pick over the beans carefully to be sure there are no pebbles or stray pieces of grit.

Put the beans in a large heavy casserole or earthenware pot. Add the onion, water and 2 tablespoons of the lard or oil. Bring to a simmer over moderate heat. Reduce the heat to low and cook, partially covered, for 1½ hours until the beans are very soft. Add the salt and continue cooking the beans for 15 minutes.

Drain the beans and puree them in batches in a food processor or blender, using a little of the cooking liquid if necessary.

Heat the remaining 4 tablespoons of lard in a large heavy skillet over moderate heat. Add the beans and cook, stirring occasionally, until they are quite dry. Taste and add more salt if desired.

Beans come in all colors, ranging from pure white to speckled yellow, pink, deep red and black. Pinto beans, red kidney beans and black beans are are readily available in the supermarket.

# Oven-Browned Potatoes with Herbs

**Serves 6**

These potatoes do not require any last-minute preparation. Simply put them in the oven 30 minutes before serving and take them out hot, crispy and browned.

> *2 pounds potatoes, of uniform size*
> *2 tablespoons (1 ounce) butter*
> *2 tablespoons vegetable oil*
> *½ teaspoon dried thyme*
> *½ teaspoon dried rosemary*
> *½ teaspoon dried oregano*
> *Salt*
> *Pepper*

Heat the oven to 375 degrees.

Peel the potatoes. Cut them in half lengthwise, quarter them and cut each quarter in half again. Blot the pieces carefully on a kitchen towel.

Melt the butter and oil in a large skillet. Add the potato pieces and the herbs. Season with salt and pepper to taste and toss until thoroughly coated. Spread the potatoes on a baking sheet. Bake in the oven for about 30 minutes until well browned and tender.

### DEEP-FRYING TIP

When deep-frying, always let the oil return to the correct temperature between batches of food. If the oil is not hot enough, the outside of the food will not seal quickly and the oil will seep into the food, leaving it soggy.

# Eggplant Fritters

**Serves 6**

You can also use this batter to make french-fried onion rings, fried shrimp or oysters and other fritters.

> *1 medium-size eggplant*
> *Salt*
> *1¾ cups all-purpose flour, plus about ½ cup for*
>   *dredging*
> *2 teaspoons baking soda*
> *2 teaspoons paprika*
> *1¾ cups cold water*
> *Oil or solid vegetable shortening, for deep-frying*

Cut the eggplant into slices ¼ inch thick. Cut the slices into thin strips. Sprinkle with salt and set on a wire rack lined with paper towels. Leave to sweat for 15 minutes, then pat dry on paper towels.

Combine 1 teaspoon of salt with the flour, baking soda and paprika in a large bowl. Stir in the water and whisk until the batter is smooth and the consistency of heavy cream.

Heat the oil or vegetable shortening to 375 degrees in a deep-fat fryer or a deep heavy skillet.

Dredge the eggplant strips with flour and shake off the excess. Dip the strips in the batter and drain off the excess batter.

Fry the eggplant, a few strips at a time, in the hot oil for about 4 minutes until the batter is crisp and lightly colored. Drain on a double thickness of paper towels. Keep the fritters spread in a single layer and serve them at once.

Drain eggplant before frying it, or it will be too watery to hold up to deep-frying.

# Apple Fritters

Serves 6

You can make fritters with almost any kind of fruit, though very juicy varieties are a little more difficult to cook. Pineapple rings and bananas, halved lengthwise, are good choices.

> *3 large cooking apples*
> *3 tablespoons sugar*
> *1 teaspoon cinnamon*
> *½ teaspoon ground cloves*
> *2 tablespoons rum or lemon juice (optional)*
>
> BATTER:
> *1 cup all-purpose flour*
> *2 tablespoons sugar*
> *½ teaspoon salt*
> *2 teaspoons baking powder*
> *¾ cup milk*
> *1 large egg, lightly beaten*
> *1 tablespoon (½ ounce) butter, melted*
> *Oil or solid vegetable shortening, for deep-frying*
> *Confectioners' sugar, for dusting*

Peel and core the apples, keeping them whole. Cut them into rings ¼ inch thick. Combine the sugar, cinnamon and cloves in a bowl and add the rum or lemon juice, if desired. Add the apple rings to the bowl, turn them in the mixture to coat and leave in a cool place for 1 hour.

Drain the apples, and pat them dry on paper towels, reserving the juices.

To prepare the batter, sift the flour with the sugar, salt and baking powder. Combine the juices from the apples with the milk, egg and melted butter. Stir the liquid ingredients into the dry ingredients, using a wire whisk.

Heat the oil or vegetable shortening to 375 degrees in a deep-fat fryer or a heavy deep skillet.

Dip the fruit in the batter and fry the rings a few at a time for 4 to 5 minutes until the batter is puffed and crisp. Drain the fritters on a double thickness of paper towels and dust with sifted confectioners' sugar. Serve at once.

# Rhubarb Fool

**Serves 8**

An old English recipe, this light and fresh-tasting dessert brings out the full flavor of the rhubarb—one of the pleasures of spring.

If you should find leaves still attached to your rhubarb, discard them; they are poisonous.

*1½ pounds fresh rhubarb, trimmed*
*1 cup sugar*
*¾ cup water*
*2 tablespoons (2 packages) unflavored gelatin*
*1 cup heavy cream, chilled*

Cut the rhubarb into 1-inch pieces. Put them in a saucepan with the sugar and ½ cup of water. Cover and cook over moderate heat for 10 minutes until the rhubarb is soft and tender. Puree the rhubarb with the liquid in a food processor or blender and leave to cool.

Pour the remaining ¼ cup water into a small saucepan and sprinkle the gelatin over it. Let the gelatin soften for 5 minutes, then set the pan over low heat and stir until the gelatin is dissolved. Let the mixture cool slightly and then fold into the cooled rhubarb.

Beat the cream with an electric mixer or a wire whisk until stiff peaks form. Fold the cream into the rhubarb. Gently turn the mixture into a serving dish and chill until set.

# Apple Brown Betty

**Serves 6**

Layers of spiced, toasted bread crumbs are combined with apples and raisins. For extra flourish, accompany it with lightly whipped cream.

> *3 slices firm-textured white bread*
> *8 tablespoons (4 ounces) butter, cut into small*
> *pieces*
> *¾ cup sugar*
> *¼ teaspoon nutmeg*
> *1 teaspoon cinnamon*
> *½ cup water*
> *½ cup raisins*
> *4 apples, peeled, cored and cut into ⅛-inch slices*
> *(about 5 cups)*

Heat the oven to 350 degrees. Butter a 2-quart soufflé dish or baking dish.

Put the bread slices in a blender or food processor and process into crumbs.

Heat half the butter in a skillet over moderate heat. Add the bread crumbs and cook, stirring, until they are toasted and browned. Combine the crumbs with the sugar, nutmeg and cinnamon.

Bring the water to the boil, add the raisins and remove from the heat. Let the raisins soak for 5 minutes and then drain.

Sprinkle a third of the crumb mixture evenly in the dish and top with half the drained raisins and half the apples. Repeat the layers, ending with a layer of breadcrumbs. Dot with the remaining butter and bake for 35 minutes until the apples are soft and tender.

# Fresh Fruit Salad

Serves 6

A freshly made fruit salad is infinitely appealing and takes very little time to prepare. The ingredients used in this recipe are generally available fresh all year round but feel free to substitute seasonal fruits that you like.

*1 pint strawberries*
*1 firm ripe banana, peeled and sliced*
*1 ripe pineapple, peeled, cored and cut into*
    *1-inch pieces*
*1 cup green or red seedless grapes*
*2 tart apples, peeled, cored and sliced*
*Lemon or lime juice*
*Sugar*

Hull the strawberries and wipe them clean with a damp paper towel. Cut them in half if they are large.

Combine all the fruit in a bowl and sprinkle with 1 to 2 tablespoons lemon or lime juice and sugar to taste. Toss gently, chill and serve.

---

### FRESH FRUIT TIPS

To ripen a cantaloupe, kiwi, pineapple or mango, enclose the fruit in a paper bag with a banana. The banana emits ethylene gas, nature's natural ripening agent, and in several days, both it and the other fruit will be luscious and ripe.

When summer berries are at their peak, freeze them individually on a baking sheet, store in a lidded container in the freezer, and add without defrosting to winter fruits.

Cut oranges or melons around the middle in a zigzag pattern and pull apart. Scoop out the fruit to add to fruit salad and use the shells as decorative containers.

A splendid pairing: fresh mint leaves and peeled, sliced oranges.

# CHAPTER 7

# PRESERVES, BUTTERS AND SAUCES

Those little extras you put on the table often spell the difference between a good meal and a memorable one. Freshly baked bread and muffins are accentuated by fruit preserves and tangy marmalades; crêpes, vegetable and egg dishes taste just a little better with a sauce; cold meats benefit from dabs of mustard, pickles and chutneys. And your table will look all the more opulent and colorful with an assortment of pretty dishes filled with preserves, pickles, fruit butters and sauces.

When you plan a special breakfast or brunch, think about the preserves and condiments as you plan the main courses. Stock up on jams and jellies, chutneys and relishes—or better still, make your own. Many can be made days or weeks in advance, particularly those that are put up with the help of a hot water bath; they keep for months. Others are best made the morning of the party, but if you have the ingredients on hand, they take only minutes to prepare—minutes that can make a big difference in the overall success of the meal.

# Tomato Sauce

**Makes about 2½ cups**

Use this basic tomato sauce when making Huevos Ran-cheros (see page 32) and Tostados with Shrimp and Crabmeat (see page 43).

*2 cups peeled, seeded chopped tomatoes*
*¼ cup finely chopped onion*
*1 small bay leaf*
*½ cup chicken broth*
*2 tablespoons (1 ounce) butter*
*2 tablespoons all-purpose flour*
*1 teaspoon sugar*
*½ teaspoon dried rosemary, basil or oregano*
*1 teaspoon tomato paste*
*Salt and pepper*

Put the tomatoes, onion, bay leaf and chicken broth in a saucepan over moderate heat. Cook gently for 30 minutes and pass through a strainer.

Melt the butter in a saucepan over low heat. Add the flour and cook, stirring, for 2 minutes. Gradually add the tomato mixture, stirring with a wire whisk until smooth. Add the sugar, herbs and tomato paste and cook the sauce gently for 15 minutes.

Season with salt and pepper to taste.

Most sauces can be made ahead of time and reheated very gently just before serving.

# Tomato and Cheese Sauce

Makes 2 cups

A sauce to serve with tortilla chips or with grilled steak or chicken.

> *1 tablespoon vegetable oil*
> *2 green peppers, seeded and finely chopped*
> *2 fresh ripe tomatoes, peeled, seeded and chopped*
> *1 cup farmer's cheese, grated*

Heat the oil in a skillet over moderate heat and fry the peppers for 2 minutes, stirring constantly. Stir in the tomatoes and cook for 1 minute. Do not let the tomatoes lose their color. Remove the mixture from the heat and let it cool. Stir in the cheese. Serve the sauce at room temperature.

# Garlic-Herb Butter with Mustard

Makes about ½ cup

Spread this savory butter between slices of a loaf of Italian or French bread, wrap it loosely in foil and bake until crisp—a welcome alternative to sweet breads on the brunch table.

> *8 tablespoons (4 ounces) butter, softened*
> *2–3 tablespoons Dijon mustard*
> *1 teaspoon lemon juice*
> *2 scallions, finely chopped*
> *1 clove garlic, finely chopped*

*2 tablespoons finely chopped parsley or fresh basil*
*Salt*
*Pepper*

Put the softened butter in a bowl, add the mustard and mix with a fork. Add the lemon juice, scallion, garlic and herbs. Mix well and season with salt and pepper to taste.

# Cheese Sauce

**Makes about 2 cups**

Rich, smooth and piquant, this sauce is an ideal complement for green asparagus and broccoli, roast chicken, poached eggs or steamed potatoes.

*3 tablespoons (1½ ounces) butter*
*3 tablespoons all-purpose flour*
*1½ cups milk*
*½ cup heavy cream*
*1 teaspoon Dijon mustard*
*½ cup grated cheddar, Swiss or Gruyère cheese*
*Salt and pepper*

Melt the butter in a saucepan over low heat. Add the flour and cook for 2 minutes, stirring frequently.

Heat the milk and cream in another saucepan over moderate heat until very hot but not boiling. Add the milk to the flour mixture gradually, stirring with a whisk until smooth. Cook gently for 10 minutes, stirring occasionally.

Add the Dijon mustard and the cheese. Stir the sauce until the cheese is melted. Season with salt and pepper to taste.

# Mexican Green Sauce

**Makes 1 1/2 cups**

Also known as *salsa verde,* this quick and easy uncooked sauce is good with chicken and fish and is used frequently with enchiladas. A bowl of *salsa verde* is as commonplace on a Mexican table as salt and pepper is on American tables.

> 10-ounce can green tomatoes (tomatillos)
> 1 small onion, finely chopped
> 1 clove garlic, finely chopped
> 2 fresh or canned serrano or jalapeño chilies,
>     drained, seeded, rinsed and chopped
> 4 sprigs fresh coriander (cilantro)
> 1/2 teaspoon salt

Put all the ingredients in a blender or food processor and process until smooth. Pour into a serving dish. Use the sauce the same day it is made.

### SOME HINTS ON CANNING

Processing preserves in a boiling water bath extends their storage time for up to a year. Use a hot water bath canner or any deep, heavy pan with a tightly fitting lid. You will need a rack to hold the jars off the bottom of the pan to prevent cracking.

Canning jars are sold with various kinds of lids and seals, and very specific instructions on how to use them. Or you can seal the jars with a double layer of melted paraffin, which will keep the contents fresh for weeks. Tightly lidded, opened jars of preserves keep well in the refrigerator for 2 or 3 weeks.

For acidic preserves such as marmalade, fragile jars can be sterilized by washing them carefully with warm water and soap, rinsing with boiling water and letting them drain dry. Fill the jars while they are still quite warm.

# Golden Nectarine Butter

**Makes about 3 pints**

A delicately spiced fruit butter that can also be made with peaches or plums. Spread it on muffins or freshly made toast.

> 4 pounds fresh nectarines, quartered (about
>    3½ quarts)
> 2 cups water
> 2 cups sugar
> ¼ cup lemon juice
> 2 teaspoons grated lemon rind
> 2 teaspoons cinnamon
> ½ teaspoon ground cloves

Combine the nectarines and water in a large heavy saucepan or casserole over medium-high heat. Cook, stirring, until the mixture comes to the boil. Reduce the heat to low and cook gently for about 10 minutes until the nectarines are tender.

Puree the fruit and juice, a batch at a time, in a blender or food processor. Return the puree to the pan. Add the sugar, lemon juice, lemon rind, cinnamon and cloves.

Cook the mixture gently over low heat for 1½ to 2 hours, stirring occasionally until thickened.

Pour the mixture into hot sterilized jars, leaving ¼ inch headroom. Wipe the rims clean and put the lids on the top of the jars. Process in a boiling water bath for about 20 minutes following reliable instructions for water bath canning. Let the jars cool undisturbed before storing.

# Homemade Mixed Fruit Marmalade

**Makes 8 8-ounce jars**

You will be amazed how much beautiful, clear, fresh-tasting marmalade can be made from just one orange, one lemon and one grapefruit. It has an excellent spreading consistency, neither too firm nor too runny.

> 1 thick-skinned orange
> 1 lemon
> 1 grapefruit
> Water
> Sugar

Cut the orange, lemon and grapefruit in half. Remove the seeds and tie the seeds into a bag made from cheesecloth. The seeds contain pectin which helps the marmalade set.

Using a sharp knife, cut through the rind and pulp of the halved fruits to make thin slivers. Measure the combined fruit and their juices and then put them in a large bowl. Add 3 times their quantity of cold water. Add the cheesecloth bag of seeds. Cover and leave at room temperature for 24 hours.

Transfer the fruit, juices and water to a 3-quart, heavy-bottomed saucepan and cook gently over low heat until the mixture is reduced to about half its original quantity.

Measure the mixture again, return it to the pan and add an equal quantity of sugar. Increase the heat to moderate and bring the mixture slowly to the boil, stirring occasionally, until the sugar is dissolved. Increase the heat to high and allow the mixture to come to the boil. Boil for about 40 minutes, stirring occasionally, until the temperature reaches 222 degrees on a candy thermometer. Remove the pan from the heat.

Discard the cheesecloth bag and skim off the surface foam. Let the mixture stand for about 30 minutes, stirring occasionally to distribute the fruit.

Pour the mixture into hot sterilized jars, leaving ¼ inch headroom. Wipe the rims clean and put the lids on the top of the jars. Process in a boiling water bath for about 10 minutes following reliable instructions for water bath canning. Let the jars cool undisturbed before storing.

# Strawberry Jam

Makes 6 8-ounce jars

Capture the flavor of summertime in this unbeatable and easily made jam.

*8 cups fresh strawberries*
*Sugar*
*Juice of 1 lemon*

Wash, hull and crush the strawberries. Measure the crushed fruit and put it in a large heavy saucepan over moderate heat.

Add ¾ cup of sugar for every cup of crushed fruit and bring slowly to the boil, stirring until the sugar has dissolved. Increase the heat to high and boil steadily until the temperature reaches 220 degrees on a candy thermometer. Stir in the lemon juice. Skim the foam from the surface.

Pour the mixture into hot sterilized jars, leaving ¼ inch headroom. Wipe the rims clean and put the lids on the top of the jars. Process in a boiling water bath for about 10 minutes following reliable instructions for water bath canning. Let the jars cool undisturbed before storing.

# Plum Conserve

Makes 6 8-ounce jars

The sweetness of plums is offset by the tang of oranges and lemons in this thick, fruit-filled conserve.

> 1 orange
> 1 lemon
> 3 pounds small firm Italian plums, halved, pitted and cut into small pieces
> ½ cup water
> 4 cups sugar
> 1 cup seedless raisins
> ¾ cup chopped walnuts

Using a vegetable parer, cut the colored part of the rind from the orange and lemon. Cut the rinds into thin matchsticks, place them in sufficient boiling water to cover and cook them for 5 minutes. Drain the rinds thoroughly.

Squeeze the juice from the orange and lemon, strain it and reserve.

Combine the plums with the orange and lemon juice in a heavy 3-quart saucepan over low heat. Add the water and sugar and cook, stirring occasionally, until the sugar is dissolved. Increase the heat to high, bring to the boil and boil for 15 minutes. Add the orange and lemon rinds, raisins and nuts and continue to boil until the temperature reaches 220 degrees on a candy thermometer. Skim the foam from the surface.

Pour the mixture into hot sterilized jars, leaving ¼ inch headroom. Wipe the rims clean and put the lids on the top of the jars. Process in a boiling water bath for about 20 minutes following reliable instructions for water bath canning. Let the jars cool undisturbed before storing.

# CHAPTER 8

# DRINKS

**B**reakfast is a time for strong, hot coffee and tea and, if you like, hot chocolate—each freshly made from top-quality ingredients. But when the clock moves along a few hours and the meal being served is called brunch, it is appropriate to concoct any number of alcoholic and nonalcoholic drinks. Guests will arrive expecting drinks such as Bloody Marys and mimosas, and delicious as these are, you might also consider serving others that especially highlight or complement the menu.

Most drinks should be mixed just before serving, although it is acceptable to prepare pitchers of Bloody Marys and daiquiris for guests to pour over ice. Chill the ingredients but do not add ice to the pitchers if you are planning to set them on the table—the ice will melt and water down the drink.

Take into account those guests who prefer drinks without alcohol as well as any children in the group by preparing a nonalcoholic punch or milk shake. And, of course, offer coffee, tea and seltzer water as well.

# Mocha Milk Shake

Serves 1

For the children (and the would-be children) at the brunch party who want something really special.

> *1 cup milk*
> *2 scoops coffee ice cream*
> *¼ teaspoon vanilla extract*
> *1 scoop chocolate ice cream*

Pour the milk into a blender. Add the coffee ice cream and vanilla. Blend at high speed for 5 seconds. Pour the mixture into a tall glass. Float 1 scoop chocolate ice cream on top and serve with a straw.

# Mexican Chocolate

Serves 2

A slightly spicy version of warming hot chocolate.

> *2 ounces unsweetened chocolate, chopped*
> *¼ cup sugar*
> *½ teaspoon cinnamon*
> *2 tablespoons hot water*
> *2 cups milk*
> *⅛ teaspoon almond extract*
> *Whipped cream (optional)*
> *Cinnamon (optional)*

Combine the chocolate, sugar, cinnamon and hot water in a saucepan. Heat over low heat, stirring, until the chocolate is melted.

Heat the milk in another saucepan over moderate heat until it is hot but not boiling. Add the milk slowly to the chocolate mixture, stirring with a wire whisk.

Add the almond extract and heat for 1 minute. Serve the chocolate in mugs and, if you like, top each one with a spoonful of whipped cream sprinkled with cinnamon.

# Spicy Iced Tea

**Serves 8 to 10**

Make this cold drink ahead of time and serve it as a refreshing accompaniment to brunch.

> *2 oranges*
> *3 lemons or limes*
> *2 sticks cinnamon*
> *1 teaspoon whole cloves*
> *¾ cup sugar*
> *2 quarts boiling water*
> *3 tablespoons loose tea, such as English breakfast or Earl Grey*

Serve hot tea in a teapot, using loose tea. Rinse the pot with boiling water to warm it up first, and let the tea steep for several minutes before pouring it. (Don't forget the strainer!)

Squeeze the oranges and 2 of the lemons into a large saucepan. Chop the rinds and pulp and put them in the pan. Add the cinnamon sticks, cloves and sugar. Pour boiling water into the pan, stir to dissolve the sugar and let the mixture stand for 10 minutes.

Add the tea and let the mixture steep for about 5 minutes, to desired strength. Strain and chill until ready to serve.

Pour into tall glasses filled with ice cubes. Cut the remaining lemon into wedges and garnish each glass with one.

# Lemonade

Serves 4

*1 cup water*
*1 cup sugar*
*5 lemons, thinly sliced, seeds removed*

The most
refreshing of all
nonalcoholic
beverages,
homemade
lemonade has
no peer.

Pour the water into a saucepan and add the sugar. Heat over medium-high heat, stirring until the sugar dissolves. Add the sliced lemons to the syrup and simmer for 5 minutes. Leave to stand for 30 minutes.

Pour the syrup into a glass pitcher filled with ice and dilute with water or club soda.

# Sangrita

Serves 6

This spicy drink is traditionally consumed between sips from a shot glass of straight tequila and sucks from a wedge of lime. Some aficionados even sprinkle salt in the tequila for a "healthy thirst." But sangrita packs a nonalcoholic punch sipped on its own, too.

*2 cups tomato juice*
*½ cup fresh orange juice*
*Juice of 2 limes*
*¼ cup finely chopped onion*
*¼–½ teaspoon Tabasco sauce*
*½ teaspoon salt*

Put all the ingredients in a blender and blend until the onion is very finely chopped. Pour the liquid into a pitcher full of ice cubes and stir thoroughly. Strain the sangrita into tall glasses.

# Brunch Bloodys

**Serves 4**

Bloody Marys are nearly synonymous with brunch and are great "eye-openers." Mix up a batch of these without the vodka for anyone who would prefer a non-alcoholic drink.

> *1 cup tomato juice*
> *Juice of 1 lemon or lime*
> *1–2 teaspoons Worcestershire sauce*
> *2–3 drops hot pepper sauce*
> *½ teaspoon celery salt*
> *5 ounces vodka*
> *Salt and pepper*
> *4 stalks celery, trimmed*

Combine the tomato juice, lemon juice, Worcestershire sauce, hot pepper sauce, celery salt and vodka in a large pitcher. Season to taste with salt and pepper and stir well.

Pour into tall glasses filled with ice cubes and garnish each glass with a celery stalk.

### WINE-BASED DRINKS

To make kir, a very popular, slightly sweet drink, combine chilled dry white wine with a drop or two of crème de cassis. A kir royale is made with champagne.

A mimosa (called a buck's fizz in England) is a mixture of chilled champagne and chilled, freshly squeezed orange juice. Although the proportions depend on your personal preference, generally they are one-third orange juice to two-thirds champagne.

# Eggnog

**Serves 12**

For a holiday brunch, your guests will appreciate a cup or two of thick, creamy eggnog.

*6 large eggs, separated*
*¾ cup superfine sugar*
*1 cup light cream, chilled*
*3 cups bourbon*
*1 cup cognac or brandy*
*2 cups heavy cream, lightly whipped*
*Grated rind of 1 orange*
*Grated rind of ½ lemon*
*Nutmeg, for dusting*

Put the egg yolks in a large bowl and beat with an electric mixer. Add ½ cup of the sugar gradually and continue beating until the mixture is light and creamy.

Stir in the light cream, bourbon and cognac or brandy. Stir in the lightly whipped heavy cream. Chill for 3 hours or stir over a bowl of ice until well chilled.

Just before serving, beat the egg whites with the remaining ¼ cup sugar to soft peaks. Fold them into the eggnog.

Transfer the eggnog to a large punch bowl. Sprinkle the surface with the grated orange rind, lemon rind and a light dusting of nutmeg. Serve in small punch cups.

As well as alcoholic beverages, brew a pot or two of coffee to serve with brunch.

# Acapulco Cooler

**Serves 2 to 4**

This is a drink for a brunch served on a hot summer day. Brilliant sprays of scarlet or pink bougainvillea are sometimes twined around a long drinking straw and put into the drink, which in Mexico is served from a hollowed pineapple or coconut shell.

For a change, substitute gin or rum for the tequila and float slices of fresh fruit in the drink.

> *2 cups unsweetened pineapple juice*
> *2 tablespoons lime juice*
> *4 ounces tequila*
> *2 cups orange juice*

Strain the pineapple juice into a pitcher of ice cubes. Add the lime juice and tequila. Strain into a large glass and fill to the top with freshly squeezed orange juice.

# Pina Colada

**Serves 4**

A favorite libation in the Caribbean, and of armchair travelers too.

> *2 cups ice cubes*
> *½ cup canned cream of coconut*
> *1 cup unsweetened pineapple juice*
> *1 cup light rum*

Wrap the ice cubes in a towel and break them up with a rolling pin. Put the ice into a food processor or blender. Add the remaining ingredients and process until the mixture is thick and smooth. Pour the drink into 4 chilled glasses, each filled with 3 or 4 ice cubes.

# Daiquiri

**Serves 4**

From sunny Puerto Rico comes a drink that has become a classic Stateside.

> 6 tablespoons sugar syrup, chilled
> 1 cup fresh lime juice, chilled
> 1 cup rum
> 3 cups cracked ice

Combine the syrup, lime juice and rum in a tall pitcher. Stir well. Put ¾ cup cracked ice in each glass and pour the daiquiri over the ice. Serve at once.

# Apricot Vodka

**Makes about 1 quart**

You will have to plan ahead for this drink as it needs to steep for about two months in a large tightly lidded glass jar or bottle.

> 1 pound dried apricots
> 1 cup sugar
> A fifth (or 750 milliliters) of vodka
> 3 tablespoons apricot brandy

Cut the apricots into small pieces and put them in a saucepan with the sugar and 1 cup of vodka. Heat over moderate heat until the liquid comes to the boil.

Transfer the mixture to a glass jar. Add the remaining vodka and the apricot brandy. Cover tightly and leave in a cool place for 2 months. Strain the liqueur into a decanter.

# INDEX